Photography for Beginners

DSLR Camera Basic Functions & Shooting Quality Photos

Dalton Fairbanks

Additionally, the information in the following pages is intended only for informational purposes and should thus be thought of as universal. As befitting its nature, it is presented without assurance regarding its prolonged validity or interim quality. Trademarks that are mentioned are done without written consent and can in no way be considered an endorsement from the trademark holder.

TABLE OF CONTENTS

*Thank you for purchasing "*Photography for Beginners: *Basic Functions of DSLR Cameras and Taking Quality Photos." This guidebook book is an excellent pocket companion for anyone who is looking to excel in photography. In this book, you will learn all about how you can use your DSLR camera to its full potential and capture high quality photos to highlight all of your favorite memories in life. Whether you are interested in capturing memorable photos of your family, of the environment around you, or of specific items or subjects, you will learn how to use your camera properly in order to get the highest quality of photos possible.*

Throughout the chapters within' this book, we will explore the basics of your new camera, as well as what each of the many modes and settings are used for. Specifically, you will learn how each setting and mode applies to your photographs, as well as how you can make sure you are using them properly in order to achieve the best possible results. In addition to learning about the basics and settings and modes, we are going to discover what equipment you can invest in that will help enhance your photography and make taking high quality photos an easier task than ever before. Then, you will get the opportunity to discover amazing advice from some of the best photographers in the industry to help you learn the ins and outs of your camera and how to improve your images. Finally, if you are interested in learning more about the video-mode on your DSLR, we have included a chapter where you can learn exactly how this mode works, and how you can take basic, high quality videos with your camera.

By the time you finish reading this book, you will feel like you are a professional photographer who truly has the knowledge and skill to capture phenomenal photographs. Whether you are just seeking to enhance your skills in order to make your family photo albums look better, or if you are looking to submit your photos to the local art gallery and eventually become a professional photographer, you will definitely feel equipped for the job. This book is an excellent resource for beginner photographers who are looking to brush off their amateur title and become true photography experts.

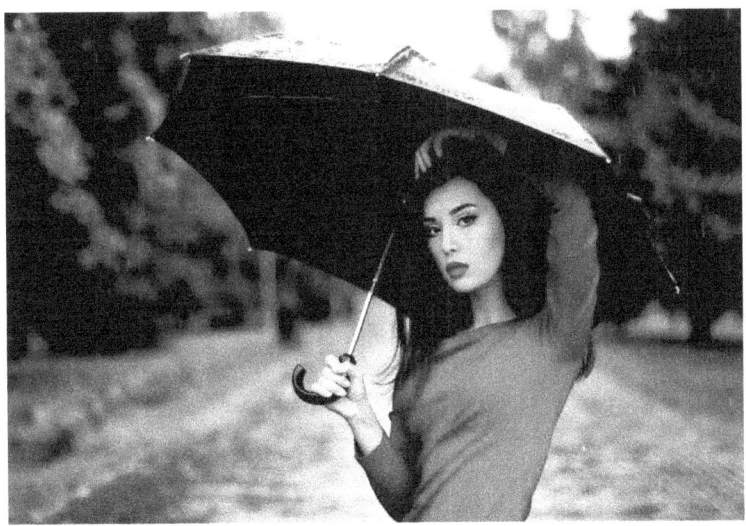

Camera Basics

The best way to truly master your craft is to start by understanding your camera. In order to truly use your camera to its fullest potential, you really need to understand the basics. By understanding the most basic elements of your camera, you will be able to understand how each part plays a role in your photographs, and how you can manipulate that part in order to take amazing photos. Because of the many settings and features offered on DSLR cameras, it is important to develop a solid foundation of these basic components before delving deeper into those more advanced features. Once you master the point-and-shoot settings of the camera, you will be able to start layering in other features and learn how to use every aspect of your DSLR in order to create amazing photographs. In order to get you to the stage where you have a solid foundation and are truly ready to move into the advanced functions, we will first learn about how your camera actually works. Then, we will explore the basic functions of the camera.

How DSLR Cameras Work

It is important to know exactly how your camera works, in order to later understand why each feature has such a large impact on the quality of your photographs. Understanding how photos are captured will help you understand what exposure is and how you can manipulate your camera to create a desirable exposure value.

DSLR (digital single-lens reflex) cameras are different from SLR cameras because of the fact that they have two viewfinders instead of just a single one. On your DSLR camera, there is the digital display that SLR cameras also feature, which shows the menus, settings, options, and more. However, in addition to that display, there is also a traditional optic viewfinder for you to look through. This viewfinder allows you to get a clearer, more "true" view of what you are photographing, and is what contributes to the high quality of photographs that can be achieved by DSLR camera users. This viewfinder allows you to look through with your own eye and get a real-time image of what your camera is looking at. Most often, they have a grid that is on (or can be turned on) that helps you line up your shots and achieve the perfect photograph. These traditional optic viewfinders were actually a major selling point on DSLR cameras, as many of their predecessors lost this when they went away from film cameras and moved into digital cameras models.

The reason why the traditional optic viewfinder became such a large point of attraction for photographers is because this viewfinder offers a much more accurate preview of the photo you are about to take. You can make sure that you align your shot perfectly, and then get an amazing shot almost every time. In general, the image you are viewing in the traditional optic viewfinder is nearly identical to the one that your naked eye would see in real life. The only difference is that this viewfinder allows for you to view the zoom-feature and such, to make sure you are getting the best possible shot.

In a basic sense, your camera works by you taking a look in your viewfinder – or at your digital display – aligning your shot, and then taking the picture. But if you look beyond the basics, and take an *imaginary look into the internal operations of your camera, you will see that a lot more actually goes into getting that perfect shot. Understanding this part of your camera is what will ultimately help you later understand features such as exposure, aperture, shutter speed, and more.*

The moment you hit the shutter-release button, light will enter through the removable or changeable lens. There, it will pass through the inner workings of the lens, and then be reflected off of a mirror, and then again off of a pentaprism. The mirror is responsible for transferring the image up to the pentaprism, which will then turn the image the right way so that you can view the image and it is not upside down. A pentaprism is a prism that has five sides and is used to deviate the beam of light that travels through your camera. This feature is found in all higher-end DSLR cameras. In the lower-end DSLR cameras, you will be more likely to find a pentamirror, which is a cheaper and lighter variation of the same tool, but it doesn't offer the same high-quality, bright image through your view finder.

So, once you hit the shutter-release button to take your picture, the shutter goes off, the mirror quickly moves away and then back into place, which causes the viewfinder to go black for a moment. When this happens, the light shines directly onto the sensor behind the mirror, which ultimately takes the picture.

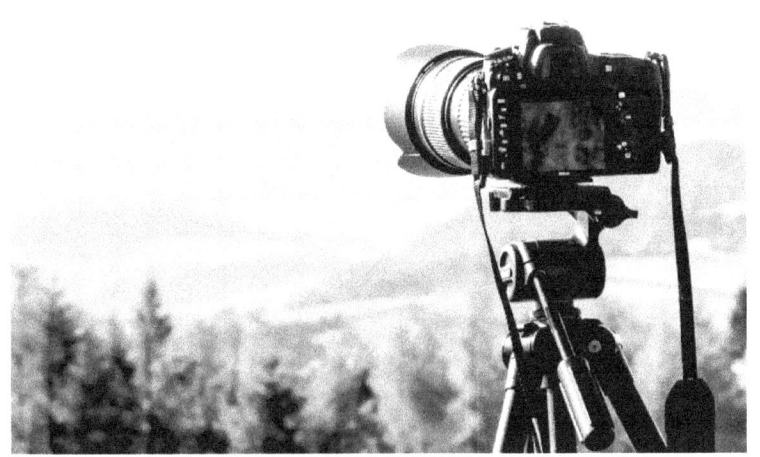

Now that you understand the way your camera works internally, you need to understand how it works externally. The external features are the part you will actually interact with in order to trigger photos to be taken and, eventually, toggle the different features and settings on your camera. There are seven basic buttons you will need to understand when it comes to navigating the external part of your camera. One of these is actually a cluster of buttons which are associated with menus and navigation of the digital operations of your camera. In addition to that cluster, there is an exposure compensation dial, the shutter-release button, the flash button, a mode dial, the ISO button, and the on/off button. Each of these buttons are important in helping you navigate your camera operations. On top of the buttons, there are also other

external features that are an important part of your camera. These include: the flash, the lens, and the lens caps.

In total, there are usually seven major buttons your camera that you will need to understand. Each of these buttons are detailed and explained in this list:

- Navigation Cluster: this isn't actually the official name of these buttons, but this generally what they are used for. These buttons help you navigate through the settings, view pictures you've taken, and change features within' your camera such as time and date, white balance, aperture, shutter speed, and more. You can typically find these buttons next to the digital display, in a circle with a main button in the center.

- Exposure Compensation Dial: this dial is usually located up next to the traditional optic viewfinder somewhere. This dial is distinguishable by a "+/-" symbol that is located on or next to it. The exposure compensation dial allows for you to make subtle adjustments to your exposure without completely altering the aperture, shutter speed, or ISO settings.

- Shutter-Release: this button is generally the easiest to recognize, next to the on/off button. This button is the large, generally bare button that is located somewhere around where your finger should naturally sit when you are operating your camera. This button is what triggers your camera to take photographs.

- *Flash Button: most DSLR cameras have a button that allow you to turn the flash on at your own discretion. This button will trigger your built-in flash to pop up and turn on. When you hit this button, your flash will work on all of your next pictures. In order to turn it off, simply press the flash closed.*

- *Mode Dial: this dial is usually located on the opposite side of the shutter-release button. It is the dial that allows you to toggle between all of the different camera modes, which we will explore deeper later on. This dial is usually recognizable by the several tiny icons that are featured on it, and a dash that is usually on your camera next to it which indicates the current mode you are shooting in.*

- *ISO: This button is usually featured by the digital display, and allows for you to quickly change your ISO settings to fix your exposure. This button will generally open up a menu from which you can select your preferred ISO setting.*

- *On/Off: this button or switch is usually pretty straight forward. It is generally the easiest button to find, next to the shutter-release button, and it turns your camera on and off.*

- *Record Button: some cameras feature a specific record button that you use when you are in video mode. This button starts and stops the recording process.*

Other External Features:

These additional features are some of the most important parts of your camera. They are important to understand, as they also play a key role in your photo-taking!

- *Lenses: we will go deeper into the different types of lenses in chapter 3, when you learn more about camera equipment, but it's important to actually understand the lens itself when it comes to photography. The lenses used with cameras are either optical lenses or assembly lenses which are used for a couple of different reasons. First and foremost, images are responsible for storing images, and most often they are also responsible for zooming in on your subject. There are many different kinds of lenses, as you will learn later. Ultimately, lenses are the part which contribute to the clarity and the quality of the photos you are taking.*

- *Flash: You are probably very familiar with the purpose of flash on a camera. Most DSLR cameras have a built-in flash that pops up when you turn it on, or pops up automatically if are using a mode that requires it to be on. However, in addition to the built-in flashes on DSLRs, you can also invest in external flashes which can be mounted to the top of your camera, generally above the viewfinder. These flashes offer various different levels of brightness and distance. You can use them in order to make your photographs brighter.*

- *Lens Caps: cameras generally have a few different caps associated with them that you use when the camera is not in use. First off, if you are storing your camera with the lens on (which is not recommended), you will need a lens cap on the side of the lens that faces away from the camera. Then, there is one that fits onto the other side, and an additional cap that locks in place over where lenses are mounted to the camera. Each of these caps are responsible for protecting your camera and lenses from damage, dirt, and wear and tear.*

Before you get into taking photographs using all of the features and settings on your camera, you should take the time to develop a true understanding of your camera itself. Most often, cameras come equipped with a lens, so you can also take the time to get to know your lens. Make sure that you never touch the glass on your lens, or the mirror in your camera or lens. If you touch them, you will introduce oils and dirt that are impossible to remove with standard cleaning tools and the debris will damage your photo quality. If this happens, you typically need to see a camera specialist to have your camera properly cleaned.

The best way to start practicing with your camera and developing a feel for these basic features is to set it in "program" mode. In this mode, everything is automatically set for you, and you can just focus on pointing and shooting photographs. To get used to everything, practice toggling through your settings, adjusting your date and time, and customizing the various features that are basic and simple to understand. Then, you can practice pointing and shooting at basic subjects, zooming in, using your flash, and toggling between the various modes and getting an idea of what each mode looks like when you shoot in it. You can also practice turning the video mode on and off.

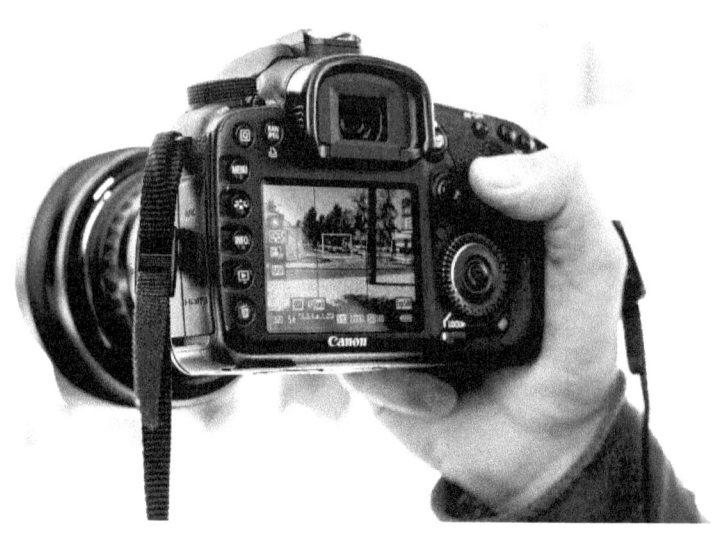

Now that you have mastered the basics of your camera, you are probably eager to start using all of the fancy modes and functions that come with it. After all, that's why most people invest in DSLR cameras, right? There are many camera modes, functions and settings available on DSLR cameras that each contribute to your ability to capture amazing quality photos. Each of these functions allows you to create the perfect image in pretty well any conditions, regardless of the visual noise, light conditions, or other factors that contribute to the quality of your photos. Instead of having to rely on chance, or be stuck with mediocre photos, you can have complete control and end up with amazing photographs.

But in order to do that, you need to understand what each function and setting contributes to, and why is it important to your photographs. You also need to understand how to work each function and setting, as well as when to choose different modes. The best way to become proficient in using these various settings and features is to practice, practice, and practice. However, it can be hard to practice if you are unaware of the basics of each feature. So, in this chapter we are going to explore the many settings, modes and features on your camera that contribute to your photographs. By the end of this chapter, you should have a fluent understanding in how to operate your camera and manipulate the settings in order to create high quality, eye catching photos that you will cherish for years to come.

Modes

There are various modes available on your camera, ranging from completely manual to totally automatic. Many DSLR cameras also have a video-mode which allows you to use your camera to film short films. If you are interested in using this mode, you can refer to chapter 6 where we go into a basic introduction of how to use this mode. Otherwise, in this section we are going to explore the ten modes that nearly every DSLR camera comes equipped with. Those modes include: program (P), shutter priority (Tv) or (S), aperture priority (Av) or (A), manual (M), auto, action mode, portrait, night mode, landscape, and macro. Each of these unique modes are important in your ability to capture phenomenal photographs in various conditions. In order to learn more about each of them, we are going to explore them in greater detail, below.

Program

On your mode dial, you will notice a capital "P", which stands for program mode. This mode is excellent when you are just looking to use your camera for point-and-shoot photography. It is very similar to auto mode, because everything is preset for you, all you do is take photos. In program mode, your camera automatically decides what the aperture and shutter speed settings should be entirely based on the amount of light that is entering your lens. In this mode, your camera will do its best to balance the aperture and shutter speed in order to create the perfect exposure for high quality photos. While you have very little control over manipulating the exposure, or other features on the image, it is still a great mode if you are just practicing how to use your camera, or aren't worried about creating absolutely perfect images. That's not to say it *doesn't have the ability to capture amazing photographs, just that it is less likely to be able to offer the same quality as you could if you were completely in control of the settings yourself. When you are learning the ropes with your camera, this can be an amazing mode to shoot in while you practice using the lens, operating between the two viewfinders, and otherwise becoming more comfortable with your DSLR camera.*

Shutter-Priority

The (Tv) or (S) on your mode dial is the symbol that represents shutter-priority mode. In this mode, your DSLR camera will automatically pick the aperture setting based on what you set the shutter speed to be. The camera decides by figuring out how much light is filtering through the lens, and where you have set the shutter speed. Then, it tries to find the perfect balance in order to make sure the aperture is going to be set just right for you to capture amazing photographs. In this mode, you get to explore and play with the shutter speed to learn how it can contribute to your photographs. However, you do risk getting overexposure or underexposure since the DSLR camera isn't capable of settings itself to the exact perfect setting in the same way you could. This is because the DSLR is being activated based on triggers within' the sensors, whereas you are actually viewing the shot with your naked eye and would have an easier time adjusting the settings properly. Still, it is a great mode to shoot in, especially while you are learning about shutter speeds and how they affect your photographs.

Aperture-Priority

This mode is represented by an (Av) or (A) on the mode dial, and it is called aperture-priority mode. As you may have guessed based on the previous mode we discussed, aperture-priority mode is the direct opposite of shutter-priority. Instead of your camera automatically choosing the aperture, this time, it will automatically choose the shutter speed. So, you can manually set your aperture to any setting you desire, and your camera will compensate by adjusting the shutter speed based on the amount of light coming through the lens. In this setting, there is much less risk of getting underexposure or overexposure. In fact, it is a very common setting for even professional photographers to shoot in, when the conditions are fair and they don't need to worry about manually manipulating each setting. In this mode, you don't have to constantly be in control of managing the exposure balance so you can pay more attention to lining up your shots and getting good quality photographs. In addition to being the most common shooting mode, it is also a great mode for learning about how aperture should be set based on your lighting conditions.

Manual Mode

This mode is called "M" on the mode dial, and it refers to manual mode. When you are in manual mode, you are in the one mode on your camera where you have full control over all of the settings and features you can use on your camera. You can determine aperture, shutter speed and ISO settings in this mode, you can manipulate your white balance, and control various other settings available on your camera. This mode is the best to use when you are in extreme light conditions and need to venture into the more extreme exposure values. This mode is excellent for having consistency between photos, and it is also a great mode to use when you are working on mastering the skill of balancing your aperture, shutter speed and ISO settings in order to get the perfect exposure on your photograph. While this isn't the most common mode for shooting in, it is the best one for learning how to manipulate every single setting in your camera to work together. It is important to know how to use this mode, for this is the mode where you will learn to master all of the fancy features that your DSLR is equipped with. Practicing in manual mode will make sure that you are fluent in understanding the exposure triangle, white balance, and more in order to have all of the settings in your camera work together to make your photographs as high quality as they can possibly be.

Auto

Simply called "auto" on the mode dial, this mode allows the camera to have total control over everything on your camera. Instead of having to focus on various settings like flash, shutter speed, aperture, ISO, or anything else, your camera will take care of all of that for you. All you have to do when you are in auto mode is point the camera and snap your picture. It operates very similar to program mode. Because of the camera having total control, there is always a high risk for overexposure or underexposure. It is not ideal to shoot in this mode on a regular basis, but it is a great mode if you just want to capture pictures and aren't worried about having the best possible quality.

Action

Action mode is usually represented by a small person who appears to be running on the mode dial. As you can probably assume, this mode is used for when you are taking pictures in action. Whether you are in action, or your subject is in action, this mode will help you get pictures that are more clear and focused than you might otherwise capture in other modes. This mode is commonly used for sporting events, parades, live events, or other situations where your subject would be moving quickly and wouldn't have time to stop and pose for the camera. Action mode is responsible for snapping pictures quickly, and having them more likely to be clear and focused on your subject.

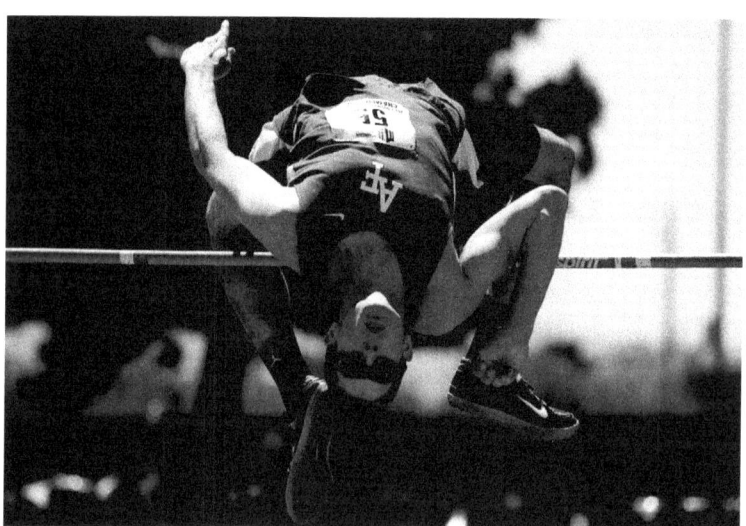

Portrait

You can recognize portrait mode as a small face on your camera, potentially with a bit of shoulders involved. This mode is used any time you are taking still shots of a main subject. In portrait mode, your main subject should be a single focus. Generally speaking, your target in portrait mode will be a small group of people closely gathered together, a single person, or perhaps an animal or an inanimate object. Either way, this mode is used when there is one (even if it is a group of closely posed things or people) major target that you are looking to focus on in your photograph.

Night Mode

This mode is generally portrayed in the same way as portrait mode, only there is a moon over the person's head. When you are shooting in night mode, you can take clearer pictures in the dark. Typically, night mode works with flash, and sets the exposure with a long shutter speed so that the camera has more time to absorb the light from the flash. When you use night mode, you get the best possible chance of having great pictures taken in the dark. Remember, you won't be able to get the same quality as you would in the light, but at least with night mode you can generally capture a great image, still. Night mode isn't only restricted to the black sky, either. Any time after dusk, you can use night mode to enhance the light quality in your photographs.

Landscape

In order to turn on landscape mode, you will switch your dial to the mountain icon. This mode is what you use when you are looking to take a photograph of any landscape. Basically, this mode will be used when you are looking to get the entire scene in the photograph, and not just a single subject. Examples include: an animal in the distance, a mountain scape, a seascape, or any other landscape style photograph. In this setting, the entire image is going to be the subject of your photograph, therefore the entire image will be clearly focused.

Macro

You can find macro on the mode dial by turning to the small icon of a flower. In macro mode, you can generate up-close pictures of smaller subjects, or smaller areas of large subjects. Generally, macro is used for smaller subjects such as insects, small flowers, foliage, small everyday items, or other smaller points of focus. However, modern photography has introduced a new passion of taking macro shots of everyday, larger items. Essentially, the photograph isolates a single area on the item and captures an extremely up close photograph of that spot. Macro is actually both a mode, and a type of lens. When you are shooting in macro mode, you can enhance the quality of your photograph and get even closer and clearer by coupling this mode with a proper macro lens. You will learn more about that type of lens in chapter 3.

Each of the ten modes on DSLR cameras has its own unique purpose that enables you to take high quality images. Most often, professional photographers gravitate towards aperture-priority or manual mode in order to capture the best photographs. However, it is important to learn each mode and its unique purpose, because each of them are important and convenient in various situations. By mastering each of the modes on your camera, you will know exactly when to use each one in order to make sure that almost every single image you capture is perfect.

Exposure Settings

There are four settings on your DSLR camera that contribute to the exposure value of your photograph. In addition to these three settings, there is a graph called a histogram that is featured on your digital display which is responsible for helping you measure your exposure value on the pictures you take. Whether you manually set these settings, or you shoot in a mode where the camera works automatically, each of these settings comes into play on every photograph you take. The three main components of exposure work together in what is professionally known as the "exposure triangle" in order to create the perfect lighting for your photographs. In order to make sure that you are creating high quality photographs every time, you will need to learn how to balance each of these to make them work in your favor. Below, we will discuss each of these settings in detail, and teach you how you can learn to operate them together in order to manipulate the perfect exposure settings for every single photograph. In the end, you will discover how the histogram works and what it tells you about your exposure settings.

A Note About Setting the Exposure Value

When you are manipulating the three main settings to create your exposure value, there is something important you need to realize. The way in which camera enters your light means that it hits each component in this order: aperture, shutter speed, ISO. However, in order to set your exposure settings perfectly, you need to work in the opposite direction of this scale. Instead, you will first set your ISO, then your shutter speed, and finally your aperture. Once you have set your exposure and are ready to take photographs, there is a final component you can factor in so that you can achieve the perfect results, if your camera isn't already getting them. This setting is called "exposure compensation", and you will learn more about it in a moment.

Aperture

The very first step in light coming through your camera is aperture, which refers to the small hole inside of your lens that allows light to pass through the camera. The aperture on your camera is very similar to the lens in your own eye: when the aperture is wider, more light passes through, and when the aperture is set to be more narrow, less light passes through.

When you are controlling aperture, you will be working what is called f-stops. These f-numbers are what represent the size of your aperture, and you will use these to manipulate the setting. The larger the number gets, the wider your aperture is, and the smaller the number is, the narrower your aperture is set. Aperture is an excellent way to control light when *you are in low light settings, but if you use it too much in higher light conditions, you will notice that the depth of field becomes incredibly shallow and detracts from the quality of your photographs. This quality of aperture is less than ideal when you are taking landscape photographs. You will need to learn how to use the shutter speed and ISO to control the light in higher light conditions.*

Shutter Speed

After passing through the aperture, light will reach the second stop in your camera which is known as the shutter. At this point, you can decide how much light will actually enter the camera itself. You can control the amount entering the camera by changing the shutter speed. Generally, you want to keep your shutter speed extremely low in order to prevent any blur from happening in your photographs. The longer your shutter speed is set to, the longer it takes for your camera to take the picture. This is because longer shutter speeds (also known as long-exposure) is a setting that is used to absorb as much light as possible. It is great for low light conditions, however in higher light conditions, having a low-exposure mode set means that if you get any camera shake, your photo will be blurry. While long-exposure is used to achieve some unique photography effects in midday, such as the soft blurry look of water in some photographs, it is generally not a setting you want to have enforced during regular photography sessions.

Your shutter speed is generally set differently based on different situations. Having your shutter speed set will help your camera know how quickly it should take a photograph, and because of this, it is ideal to use it to manipulate the speed of your camera based on what you need. For example, if you are shooting an action photo shoot you will want to have your shutter speed set to just a fraction of a second (as low as 1/4000, even) in order to make sure that you capture moments without missing them, and without blur. In action shoots, people often also use "burst mode" in which the camera takes several photographs in a single click of the button. This enables photographers to almost always capture the perfect photograph, even if the others turn out to have blur or other undesirable qualities to them. If you were taking a still shot at night, however, you would want to have your shutter speed set longer (even around 30 seconds) so that your camera has the opportunity to absorb more light. How long you set the shutter speed will really depend on how much light you have available, and whether or not your subject will be moving around a lot. A good tip to prevent camera shakiness when you are shooting long-exposure photographs is to use a tripod to stabilize your camera. If you don't have one available, it is recommended that you rest your hands or camera up against something more stable – such as a tree or a fence post – in order to prevent shakiness and burry photographs.

ISO

The final stage of the exposure triangle is ISO. This is the last part of light entering through your camera before the picture is taken. So, after the light passes through the aperture, then the shutter, it reaches a sensor which is where the ISO setting comes into play. Generally, the ISO setting will be the first thing you change when you are setting the exposure for your photographs. This allows you to set the basis for the light-balance on your camera. It is important to keep your ISO as low as you possibly can when you are setting it, because the higher it is set, the more "grain" or digital noise will enter your photograph. Lower settings reduce or completely eliminate this digital noise and create a clearer picture overall.

Exposure Compensation

In addition to the main three settings (aperture, shutter speed, and ISO) there is a final setting that you can refer to when you are setting the exposure on your camera. Sometimes, you get the above three set just perfectly, but for one reason or another you just don't have the exact exposure you are looking for. When this happens, you can use the exposure compensation dial in order to adjust the overall settings and create a brighter, or darker picture depending on what you need. Remember, the exposure compensation dial is represented by a "+/-" symbol and is generally located near the traditional optic viewfinder. You can simply turn it in the plus or minus direction depending on what you need, and the overall settings of your exposure will increase slightly, or decrease slightly. Using this dial, you can manipulate the perfect light settings for your photograph.

Exposure Triangle

When you are reading photography books, speaking to other photographers, or taking photography workshops, you will most likely hear about something called the "exposure triangle". The exposure triangle is a method for people to explain the way the three components *of exposure work together in order to make the overall light quality in your photographs. Essentially, whenever you change one of the settings, the other two need to adjust in order to keep the exposure balanced. For example, the higher you set your aperture, the faster you will want your shutter speed, and the lower you will probably want your ISO setting. On the other hand, if you were to turn the aperture down, you would want the shutter speed to be longer, and maybe have the ISO turned up. Ultimately, there is a perfect balance that needs to be achieved in order to get the best quality of lighting in your pictures. When you change one part of the triangle, the other two will need to be adjusted accordingly.*

There are two phrases you need to learn for when you are using exposure triangles: exposure value (sometimes called EV) and stops. The exposure value directly refers to the specific value of the combined aperture, shutter speed, and ISO settings. The stops refer to the amount of light that is reaching the sensor. F-stops, which correlate with aperture and are used when you are setting the aperture of your camera, can be extremely confusing for beginner photographers. F-stops do not run in a sequence that makes sense to an untrained mind: instead of increasing numbers based on the numbers themselves, it increases numbers based on the doubling of square roots. The easiest way to use F-stops is to remember the F-Stop count. The F-stop count is as follows: f/1.4, f/2, f/2.8, f/4, f/5.6, f/8, f/11, f/16, f/22, f/32.

Essentially what you need to know about the exposure triangle is that every time you change a setting, you need to adjust others in order to compensate for the change. Through this compensation, you will achieve clear, focused pictures. If you are not balancing the three settings, you will either get pictures that are underexposed, overexposed, or completely out of focus. You can play around with where your settings will need to be, knowing that the higher your aperture is set, the more focused it will be on a single subject, and the lower it is, the easier it will be to focus on the entire scene. However, ultimately the settings are going to need to operate best with the light conditions around you in order to achieve the best quality photographs.

Histogram

The final part of the exposure puzzle is the graph that is called a histogram. The histogram on your camera is the graph that is featured on the digital display whenever you take a photo. This graph will give you information explaining how well the quality of your image is, particularly based on the lighting and exposure in your photo. Ideally, you want your histogram to be even and centered. If any part of the histogram is touching any of the edges, you will have loss of detail in that particular area of the photo. When the graph lines touch any of the edges, this is called "clipping". There are two specific types of clipping: first there is what is called highlight clipping, which means that there was too much white in the photograph so you have lost detail to the whiteness. The second type is called shadow clipping, which means there were too many shadows in your photo and you lost detail to those. In either instance, you can fix the quality of your photograph by adjusting the exposure appropriately: allowing more light in shadow-clipped photographs, or less light in highlight-clipped photographs.

The histogram on your camera is an incredibly important part of your exposure settings. This graph is able to give you detailed information on how you can achieve the highest quality photographs, and what you need to alter if you aren't already. When you are learning to take good photographs, and even later when you are a pro, this histogram will give you all of the information you need to know about the exposure you have set for your photos.

White Balance

In addition to the exposure values and the histogram that goes along with those, there is a final part of your photography that you can control. The white balance setting is found in your menu, and helps you ensure that your camera is set to pick up the truest colors from your surroundings. When your white balance isn't set right for your particular conditions, you may notice strange color tinging in your photograph. To fix this strange tinge, all you have to do is enter your settings and manipulate your white balance to remove these tinges and have a photograph that has truer color.

Now that you have a detailed understanding of the modes and the features on your camera, it is time for you to practice playing around with it! In order to do so, you should set your camera to manual mode and practice altering the exposure triangle values in order to achieve the best exposure possible. This is essentially the last part of the puzzle to *master in order to revoke your title of amateur photographer and start stepping into the world of professional photography!*

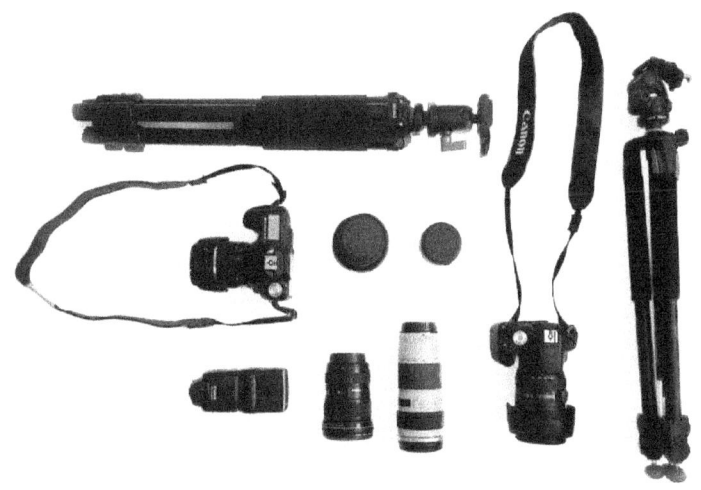

When it comes to photography, there are infinite amounts of equipment you can purchase that will contribute to your photographs. This equipment does anything from adding manual filters to your photographs, to making it more convenient to take certain photos. When you are just starting out, it may seem intimidating to see all of the equipment you can purchase. Rest assured, even most professional photographers don't stock up on the majority of those tools. While they are fun, and can offer incredible features to your photography, many cater to specific niches. Later, once you pick a niche (if you do) you might consider investing in equipment that will help you take better photos in those particular conditions. In the meantime, you should simply focus on using your own camera and what it came with.

Still, you may be interested in knowing what the best equipment is for beginners to invest in. In no particular order, we have grouped together the best equipment you should consider purchasing when you are taking up photography. There are several care and maintenance pieces that are excellent to have on hand in order to make sure you are taking the best possible care of your equipment, as well as some additional pieces that you can invest in to make your photography more enjoyable, or more convenient.

In this chapter, we have created a list that features all of the most important pieces of equipment that you should consider getting as a beginner photographer. Each of these pieces will contribute greatly to the care of your equipment, the quality of your photos, and the ease with which you can capture your photos. As we mentioned, you don't necessarily need all of these pieces, but it is a good idea to consider them nonetheless. Many of these items actually are the basics that most photography professionals ensure to keep around in order to contribute to the quality of their photographs and the care of their equipment.

Cleaning and Care Equipment

One of the most important parts of owning a camera, as with anything, is making sure that you are taking proper care of it. This includes proper storage, as well as proper cleaning methods. If you are going to invest in any equipment for your camera, it is recommended that you focus on this list first, and then explore other items later. The following items are excellent for helping you keep your camera in brand-new condition so that it is always ready to take the highest quality photos with you:

Microfiber Cloth

Microfiber cloths should be the only thing you use to wipe your camera clean. They are excellent at eliminating dust and dirt that may build up, without leaving behind any lint or residue. It can be beneficial to keep a clean microfiber cloth, similar to the ones you use to clean glasses, handy at all times.

Compressed Air

Cans of compressed air are great to keep handy in order to blow difficult dust out of buttons and hard-to-reach areas on your camera. When you have dust on your camera, especially inside, it can damage the quality of your photographs.

Good, Tough Camera Bag

DSLR cameras have a ton of odds and ends that go along with them. When you are storing or transporting your camera, you will need to have a high quality camera bag to keep it in. A good camera bag should offer some shock support in case it gets bumped around, as well as plenty of compartments to keep all of the different pieces in. This should be one of the first investments you make, as you don't want your brand new camera sitting out in the open risking damage!

Lenspen

These cleaning tools are excellent for properly cleaning the lens and removing smudges. It can be nearly impossible to do this with basically any other cleaning element, but having a dirty lens can really destroy your pictures. Lenspens allow you to clean your lens properly and continue taking photos right away, rather than having to get your camera professionally cleaned.

External Equipment

There are many pieces of equipment you can purchase to use with your camera. These items make it convenient and easier to take better quality photos. While they are not as necessary to you as the cleaning and care equipment is, they are still important if you want to grow as a photographer.

Memory Cards

Most cameras won't even save your pictures if you don't have memory cards. Some won't even take pictures to begin with, if you don't have one installed. Typically, you buy a memory card at the same time as you buy your camera. Most often your camera will come with one included in the package. If you don't have one, you'll need to get one. It is recommended to get at least a 32gb memory card, but the more storage the better. Memory cards that are too small won't be able to hold many high quality photographs, and you'll run out of space quickly.

In addition to memory cards, you can also purchase external hard drives. These are great for storing your pictures on so you can easily transport them and view them from any device at any time. There are many different sizes of external hard drives that you can buy, so you'll just have to shop around and find one that works best for you. Typically, if you are going to spend money on one, you should invest in at least 1 terabyte.

Spare Battery

If you use your camera a lot, there's a good chance you'll wear down the battery quickly. Having a spare battery is an excellent opportunity to keep yourself from running out of battery and having to stop shooting just because your camera has died. Instead of finding yourself in this situation, you should invest in a spare battery. Keep both charged and on-hand at all times. This way, you can take as many photographs as you want and never have to worry about losing power.

Remote Shutter Release Cable

These cables are incredible for photographers, especially if you are planning on doing a long exposure photograph. If you are planning on doing any photography with exposure longer than 30 seconds, you'll need one of these. They are also great for taking photos when you are further away from your camera.

Tripod

These are one of the most basic pieces of camera equipment, but are still just as important. Tripods help you line up the perfect shot and keep your camera completely still while you are taking pictures. When you have your camera on a tripod, you don't have to worry about getting any shakiness in your photograph. This is even better when you are shooting long-exposure pictures where shaking can greatly damage the quality of your photograph.

Lenses

One of the most popular reasons people purchase DSLR cameras is because of the endless lenses there are to purchase. Each lens does something different, from manually adding a filter to your photographs, to having different zoom capabilities. Generally, you start out with a basic lens that zooms from 55mm-250mm. However, there are many more that you can purchase in order to get better photographs, depending on the conditions you are taking pictures in. Below are the best lenses for those who are just starting to build their collection. While you won't need every single kind of lens here, it does help to understand what each one does and why it can be useful.

Standard Lens

These mid-range lenses typically focus around 50mm. They feature an angle view that portrays an image approximately the same as a human's eye would, helping the photos appear more "natural". Generally, standard lenses have a fixed focal length and a wide aperture, meaning they operate exceptionally in low light situations. They are great for landscapes, portraits, and taking candid shots.

Macro Lens

These lenses are designed specifically for up-close photography. They are constructed differently inside which causes them to create an incredible sharpness and contrast in photographs. The photos they produce are extremely eye-catching and impressive. These lenses are extremely useful in close-range photography, and are generally used for photographing things such as: insects, animals and plants. They have also become popular for taking incredibly details photographs of everyday items.

Telephoto Lens

Opposite of a macro lens, the telephoto lens allows you to take incredible shots of items that are far away from you. They magnify to an extremely high level, allowing for you to shoot photographs of subjects that are in the moderate to far distance. These lenses tend to be much larger and heavier than other lenses, though they are slowly evolving to be more compact and manageable. These photography lenses are popular for shooting all sorts of photographs where you can't get up close to the subject. Some examples include wildlife and sporting events. They also tend to be used when taking portraits, as a moderate telephoto lens can provide natural, undistorted perspectives.

Wide Angle Lens

These lenses have a short focal length. They provide an angle view that is beyond what a standard lens provides, which allows them to capture

42

much more of the scene in front of you in just a single shot. There are some extremely wide angle lenses that are known as fisheye lenses, which capture approximately 180 degrees of photograph. Fisheye lenses make intriguing, somewhat abstract photographs that are extremely interesting to look at.

These lenses are great for shooting landscape photographs, as well as cramped interiors, and other subjects that wouldn't otherwise fit into a normal lens's field of view. Fisheye lenses are even better at taking extremely wide photographs, and have become popular for photographing subjects such as action sports.

Specialist Lens

There are a wide number of other lenses available out there that are considered specialist lenses because they fulfill fascinating different techniques. Some of these specialty lenses include: tilt and shift lenses, soft-focus lenses, and infrared lenses.

External Flash

Another piece of equipment that is commonly forgotten about by beginner photographers is the external or removable and changeable flash feature. While most come with built-in flash, there are still many external flash items you can purchase yourself. The different types include:

Dedicated Camera Flash

A flash unit that fits onto the hot shoe of your camera and communicates directly with your camera to achieve the proper light settings.

Macro Ring Light Flash

A small circular flash that is used when taking macro photographs in order to get the perfect lighting when shooting close-up detailed photos.

Hammerhead Flash

Separate from the camera, this flash unit is common in event photography because it puts out a higher light than other flashes and provides a better angle and grip than other types.

In addition to all of the equipment you have seen here, including many of the special items we've featured, you may also discover several other pieces of equipment that interest you. While most are unimportant to the quality of your photos, many can help you manipulate your photos to achieve certain angles, looks, or other interesting features. While most professional photographers agree that you should focus on having minimal equipment as a photographer, you may still be interested in exploring these options and finding ones that suit your particular desires to help you achieve the look you are wanting to achieve.

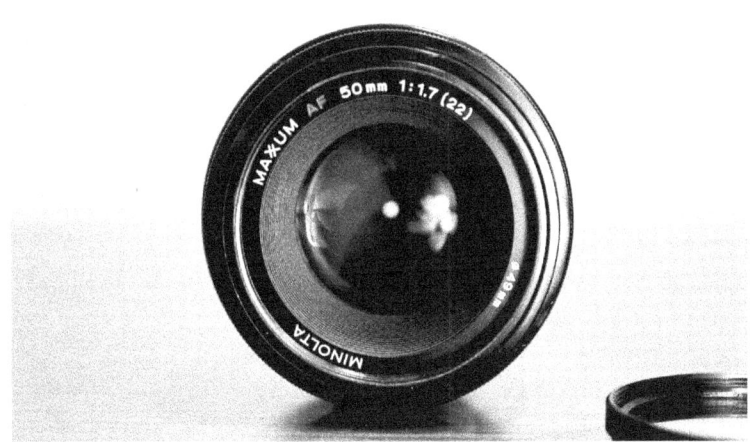

Getting Good Images

There are many contributing factors when it comes to getting an image that is high quality. For starters, you need to understand how to use the aperture, shutter speed, ISO and modes which we previously talked about. By understanding how to use these on your camera in order to produce good photos, you will have the basics down to help you create high quality photographs. However, there is much more to learn, as well. In this chapter, we will provide you with two things: first, you will learn how the basics of using aperture, shutter speed, ISO and modes on your camera. Then, we will provide you with a cheat sheet of things you should remember and test out when you're practicing taking photographs. The best way to get incredible at taking high-quality photographs is to practice. The more you play with your camera, the more comfortable you will become with it, and the better your pictures will turn out as a result.

The Basics to Capturing Incredible Photographs

In order to produce high quality images, you will first need to pick which mode you want to shoot in. Depending on what setting you are in, you can choose the mode most appropriate to your settings. In chapter 2, you can review the detailed guide to each mode and its purpose. Pick one that best suits your current situation.

The best way to get the most control over your photograph is to enter the manual setting. The rest of this tutorial is going to be based on the manual setting, as this is where you will be able to customize every element of your photo and have greater control over the results. In other modes, you are limited in what you can alter in order to produce your photographs.

Once you are in manual mode, you need to start focusing on how you will set your exposure. As a new photographer, it may take a few test photographs in order to really get your settings correct. You can start by fixing your ISO settings to match your current lighting situation. So, in order to adjust the ISO, you first need to establish whether you are in dark, dim, or light settings. The darker your surroundings are, the more you will have to increase the ISO in order to create a light base for your photographs. However, you need to be careful when increasing your ISO because the higher it is, the more grain (or "digital noise") will be in your photograph. In lighter conditions, you can lower your ISO.

Once you have your ISO base set up, you can fix your shutter speed. The shutter speed will need to be set in order to help you capture enough light to produce a quality picture, without having it set to too long. The longer your shutter speed is, the longer the photograph will take to process, which means there is more opportunity for blur in your photograph. If you are doing long-exposure photos, or photos with long shutter speeds, it is a good idea to use a tripod and set your camera in a sturdy area so there is no blur as a result of this setting.

In order to pick the right shutter speed, you will need to consider your lighting once again. This is easiest to do if you are using a digital display in the beginning, though eventually you will understand it and it will be easier for you to do it without having to think about it as much. So, the shutter speed needs to be quicker the brighter it is, and longer the darker it is. There are several settings for the shutter speed, typically ranging from 1/8000 (which means 1/8000 of a second) to 1/4 of a second and lower. The higher the number is, the quicker your shutter speed will be, and vice versa.

Aperture is the final setting you will need to fix in order to get your photographs perfect. With aperture, it is rated in f-stops, so you will notice that it says f/number. The numbers range from 1.4 to 32, and tell you how large the opening is for the aperture. When you are playing with aperture, you will also be playing with the depth of your camera, so you have to be careful to make sure that you aren't affecting the quality of your photo by losing depth. If you are taking photographs, generally you will want to use a lower aperture for a shallower photograph, such as if you are taking a photograph of a cereal box or something flat. Then, you'll want to use higher apertures for images where you require more depth. The higher your aperture, however, the softer your image will be, also. So, you'll need to play around and find what works most for your current photography settings.

While it might seem easier to set your camera in automatic modes, or rely on the built-in flash to help you get better lighting in your camera, it's not beneficial to you as a photographer. Relying on these conveniences can really inhibit your photography skills, as well as they will not serve you in certain situations where these conveniences don't work. You really need to spend time making sure that you learn these different tactics in order to expand your photography skills and take photographs that you can be proud of.

Tips, Tricks, and Photography Secrets

In addition to understanding how to set up for a basic shot, there is more for you to know and consider when it comes to taking high quality photographs. In this section, we are going to teach you tips, tricks, and some of the best photography secrets in order to make sure you are taking professional-quality photographs in no time.

Use Natural Light Whenever Possible

Even though there are many fancy and incredible lighting systems out there, none of them compare to natural light. If you are looking to get the highest quality photographs, you should do your best to take photos when there is natural light present. This way, you don't have to compensate with your exposure and can capture better images, easier.

In your cameras viewfinder, you should see a grid that contains nine boxes. If not, you can typically turn this on in your settings. Once it's on, you can use this grid to help you create the most incredible images. In order to use this grid to help you properly set up your photograph, all you need to do is align the main focus point with one of the intersections on the grid. This method is used by many photographers in the industry, and time and again has created many wonderful photographs.

Remember White Balance

White balance is a setting on the camera that many people forget to use. This setting is similar to color temperature scales. Typically, if you are getting images that are producing strange color overcasts, you need to change your white balance in order to create a more balanced tone of colors. Adjust your white balance whenever you notice a trend of unsightly colors that are staining your photographs. You will need to play around with it to find what works best for your current setting.

Practice Mastering Exposure

This word comes up often, and is actually the basis for photography for the most part. Without proper exposure, your photographs will turn out too white or too dark, and this will ruin your photograph's quality. While it might seem tedious and sometimes a little overwhelming, it is important to take the time to master exposure with your camera. The better you get with using exposure to your benefit, the better your photographs will get, also.

Stabilization

Most cameras have a stabilizer, but they can only do so much. Especially with beginners, it can be common to find images where camera shake has caused blurs or distortions in the image. If you are using a camera, especially in long-exposure modes, you will want to use a tripod in order to get the best quality photograph that isn't affected by camera shake. You should also use the stabilizer on your lens or camera in order to get the best, stable photograph.

Post-Photo Editing

This is one of the most exciting parts of photography that many beginners forget about. Being able to edit your photos after taking them is exciting. You get to play with the color tones, the focus, the angles, and so much more. It is suggested that you purchase a high quality photo editor in order to be able to play around with the editing portion of your photography.

Exposure Compensation

In addition to setting the exposure yourself, there is a dial on your camera that is typically marked with a "+/-" symbol. This dial is used to compensate for the exposure of your photograph. So, if you have it set properly but are consistently getting small botches in your exposure, you can use this dial to increase or decrease the exposure slightly, in order to contribute to the quality of your photographs.

Enjoy Yourself

While you are taking the time to learn this exciting new hobby, you should also remember to enjoy yourself! It can be easy to get caught up in all of the different do-this's and don't-forget-that's. Remember, photography is supposed to be fun and expressive. Take your time, practice your craft, and enjoy yourself! The more you practice and have fun with it, the better your image quality will be over time. Take your time, and go easy on yourself. You'll be shooting with the professionals in no time. And on that note, even professionals make mistakes. So, it can be a great benefit to you early on to learn to love the mistakes you make and learn to laugh at the ones that are crazy.

Eliminate Shutter Lag

Shutter lag is that moment when you press the button and the shutter takes a while to respond, despite it being set at a specific setting. The easiest way to compensate for this is to half press the shutter release button, then focus your image and press the rest of the way when you are ready to take the image. This way, your camera should respond almost immediately, or at least however you have set it to respond.

Back Up Everything

A major mistake people make is not backing up their photographs. You should make it a habit early on to back up every single photograph you take and edit you make. This is where having an external hard drive can come in handy. Having backups helps make sure you never lose all of your incredible art. Plus, if you are going to be a professional photographer, backups means you will never lose your clients product. It is very important that you back up your camera constantly. You should do this by plugging your SD card into the computer and uploading all of your pictures into your computer, and then either putting them onto an external drive, or saving them to a cloud storage platform. Either way, it is important that all of your images are backed up on a regular basis, in case anything ever goes wrong. That way, you'll never lose your images.

Photograph Anything

Especially as a beginner, the best way is to take a picture. If you aren't sure of what to photograph, or when, just take as many pictures as you desire. This way, you will almost definitely get an amazing photograph, and you won't have missed the best moments. Whenever you're in doubt, just snap a picture. In the worst case scenario, you just delete it later on, if it didn't turn out how you desired.

Don't Feel Obligated to Be Fancy

This goes for equipment and for photographs. When you are taking photographs, it is not necessary to have all of the big fancy equipment.

You don't need the best camera, or the best quality lenses, or anything like that. As long as you have a good camera and a good lens, and you take your time and learn to use them to the best of their (and your) ability, you will be able to take great pictures. Anything that doesn't turn out incredible can be edited later on! This is the same case with taking photographs. Professionals, or people who have been photographing for years may be more artsy or creative with capturing their shots. You don't need to be. All you need to do is find a subject that you like, and practice taking photographs of it. Some of the best photographs are the most simple, common-sense type photographs of everyday objects that we wouldn't even think of otherwise. Don't feel like you absolutely have to be wildly creative and imaginative in order to take amazing photographs. It simply isn't true.

Getting The Frame Right

When you're practicing getting the right photos, or even when you're just taking photographs of an event, you don't need to feel obligated to be in manual all of the time. Even many professional photographers don't use manual too often. While you do need to understand how the setting works, since the others aren't always efficient in various settings, you don't need to use it all of the time. Instead, use a setting like aperture-preferred, shutter-preferred, or program, and just practice lining up the shots properly. Getting your shot lined up is just as important as understanding exposure, if not more since exposure can be automatically dealt with but the alignment cannot. So, make sure you spend an adequate amount of time practicing aligning your photographs properly.

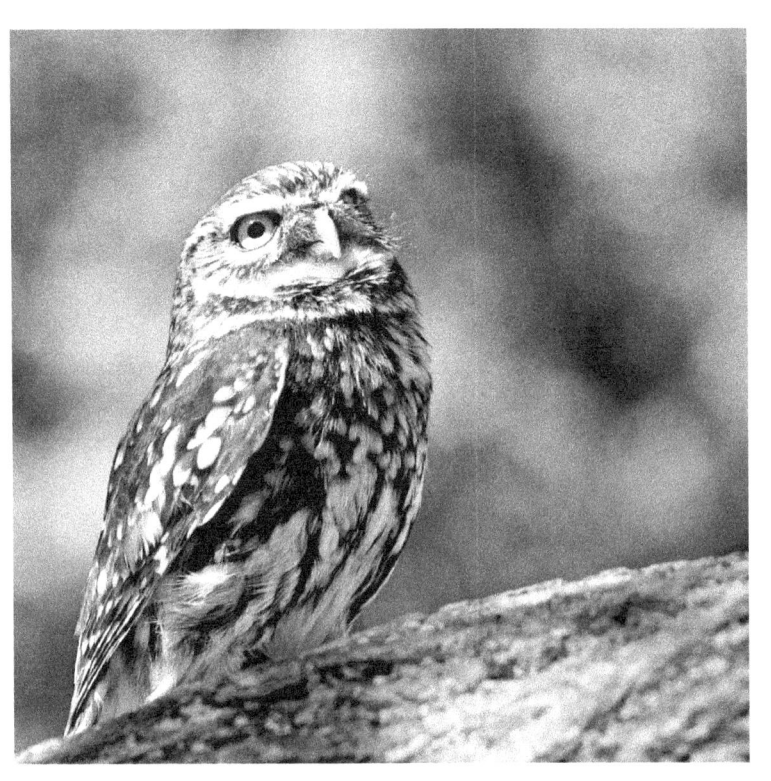

Photography Workshops or Groups

While there are many schools that teach photography, it isn't necessary to spend the money to attend one if you don't want to, or can't afford to. Photography workshops are often considered to offer more value in the long run, especially since you can pick your focus and the speed at which you practice. If you don't want to attend either but would still like support, there are often photography groups in various locales that take on new members and are happy to show them the ropes and help offer constructive criticism so you can understand where you can focus on practicing more.

Try to Get a Good Photo Every Month, and A Great One Every Year

No photographer can possibly get the best photo every single time. No matter how professional you are, you are not always going to wind up with amazing photographs. So, as a hobbyist, it is reasonable to aim for a single good photo each month, and one great one every single year. By eliminating the stress of making every single photo a great shot, you increase your odds of making them fairly good or admirable almost every time. Take the pressure off and enjoy yourself! Your work will truly represent that new found relaxation.

Have Strong Visual Anchors

Your photographs should generally have a single strong visual anchor. Even if this anchor is an entire forest, there should be a certain area of the photograph that your eye is drawn to: maybe a tree leaning a certain way, or a small clearing that looks unique or otherwise attractive. Having a visual anchor that attracts the eye is a great way to increase the desirability of your photographs. It eliminates the distraction and confusion that could be related with your photos, and makes them more impressive to look at.

Don't Limit Yourself

It isn't necessary to take one or two photographs of a scene and then move on. You can easily take several photographs of a scene from various different angles without having to worry about taking "too many". The more photographs you capture, the more likely you will find one that you truly love. Don't worry about working all of the different angles and getting several tens of photographs of a single scene. This is totally normal, even for professional photographers. You never know which one will turn out the best until you get a chance to look at them and edit them later on. So, don't rob yourself of the perfect shot. Take several!

Practice Daily Instead of Weekly

Instead of practicing for several hours on a given day, try practicing for a few minutes each day. Of course, you can plan outings where you will photograph longer, but in general you will benefit more from practicing each day than you will from practicing once or twice a week. The more you are exposed to your camera and the practice of taking photographs, the better you will get behind the shutter and the quicker your skill will improve.

Print Your Work

As a photographer, it is easy to stack up several hundreds of photographs and never look at them again. Instead of letting your beautiful art go into hiding on a disk drive somewhere, make it viewable at a moment's notice. Print off your favorite work and display it prominently. Whether you make your work viewable in your home, or you make scrap books with your photographs, you should make sure that all of your favorites are printed and easy for you to see. This way, you can share them, show them to friends and family, and see them at any time. Art work deserves to be displayed!

Don't Favor Certain Angles

It can be easy to find a comfort zone and get stuck in it. Many people prefer shooting in just horizontal angles. However, it is a good idea to shoot both horizontal and vertical photographs. Both are beautiful, and it can be beneficial to practice both so you are able to effectively make either angle look amazing.

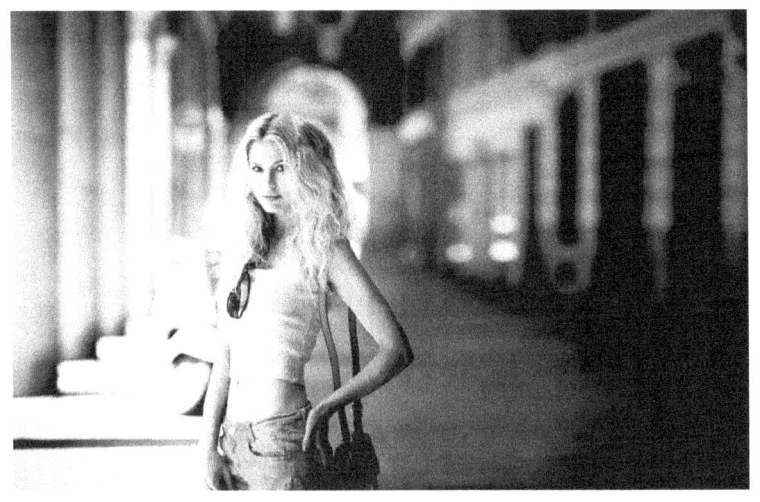

Invest in Books, But Only Valuable Ones

Photography books are an incredible place to learn information about how to shoot better photographs. Even better are books that specifically correlate to your exact camera model, since they will be customized to the equipment you are working with. If you are going to invest in anything, many people suggest investing in a good quality photography book, even in favor of new camera equipment. Books have a lot to offer, and are incredible teachers when it comes to learning a new craft. You can always re-read a book when you need help, in order to increase your skill and become a better photographer. However, you shouldn't waste money on a book you won't reread. If you are going to buy a photography book, make sure it is one you can (and will) refer back to any time you need, in order to find out the information you need to know.

Photograph Your Loved Ones

Many people invest in photographs and then feel compelled to get people to model for them, or to only photograph items or landscapes. Don't forget that your family and friends make amazing models, and having them in your photographs will make for a great memory in years to come. When you are at a gathering, hanging out with friends, or otherwise spending time with loved ones, it is a great time to capture those amazing memories as well as practice your skills. You can even specifically ask them to model for you while you are practicing, if you want.

Start a Photography Blog

There are many great values to having a photography blog for when you are learning to photograph. First off, it is a wonderful opportunity to share your photos with your family and friends, and anyone else who might be interested in your work. Second, it is a wonderful way to connect with other photographers and share your artwork with them. You can maybe even return the favor and explore their artwork, too! And third, it is a great place to get constructive criticism from other photographers who might be willing to share tips, techniques and tricks with you! In addition to all of those wonderful perks, you can also scroll through your posts and easily see just how much your skill has increased as you practice more and more!

Make Your Own Tips

While its highly beneficial to learn from others, there's nothing more profound than your own experience. When you are learning a new skill, such as photography, it can be very helpful to have a notebook handy where you can jot down notes, tips and tricks that you learn along the way. This way, you have all of the best information you have learned along the way available to you at any time. These books can be handy to look back on later when you are having a hard time, need help troubleshooting, or would like to remember what has worked best for you in past circumstances. It is a good idea to keep this notebook handy any time you are taking photographs, working with your camera, editing photographs, or otherwise doing photography-related tasks. This way, you get all of the information relevant to your new skill written down *and can avoid going through the same troubles again in the future that you may have already experienced.*

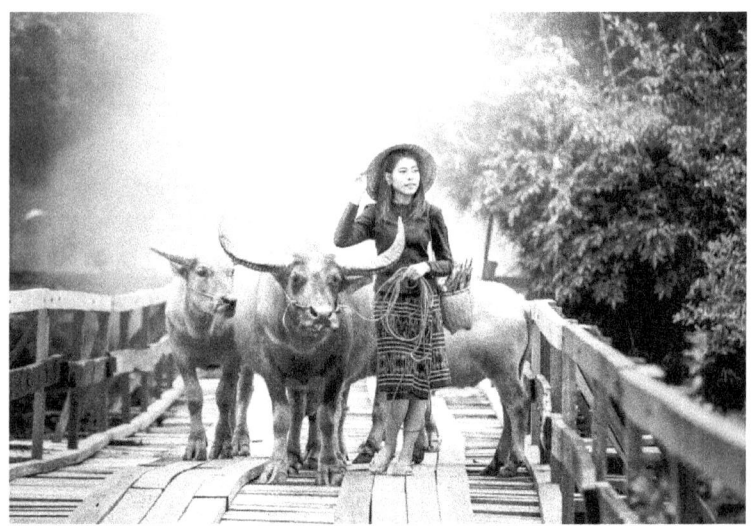

So, now you have learned all about how to use your camera, and you've seen the tips, tricks and secrets on how to capture the best photographs. But now what? This chapter is dedicated to giving you inspiration on where and when you can practice taking photographs. Each place and time in this checklist is there to help you learn to shoot in all conditions so you can truly master the art of photography.

Checklist:

The most important part of learning to take pictures effectively is doing them in different settings and conditions. So, in this checklist we have included a variety of places you should practice taking photographs, as well as a variety of times you should practice. Finally, we have also included a variety of subjects you can practice on! This way, you get well-rounded with your skills and become a photography master.

Times

- Early morning

- Afternoon

- Evening

- Night

- Bright Day

- Cloudy Day

- Dark Sky

Places

- In an artificially lit room

- In a poorly lit room

- Outside near a body of water

- In a forested area

- In an open field

- On a crowded street

- At a gathering of people

- A sporting event

- A concert or live event

Subjects

- A single person

- A group of people

- A single person in a crowded place

- An animal

- A landscape

- A plant, flower, or leaf

- An insect

- The sky

- Clouds

- A body of water

- An inanimate object

While the list of things you could photograph in various settings is exhaustive, the above list will help you establish your skills in a variety of areas. Ultimately, the best way to get practice, is to just take photographs. The more you practice, the more you are going to be exposed to different settings, with physical surroundings, lighting and subjects. This is what will help you become fluent and well-versed in taking photographs of anything, at any time. The more you practice on a wide variety of subjects in a wide variety of conditions, the better your photographs are going to look each time, and the more knowledge you will have about how to prepare your camera in order to get the best shots.

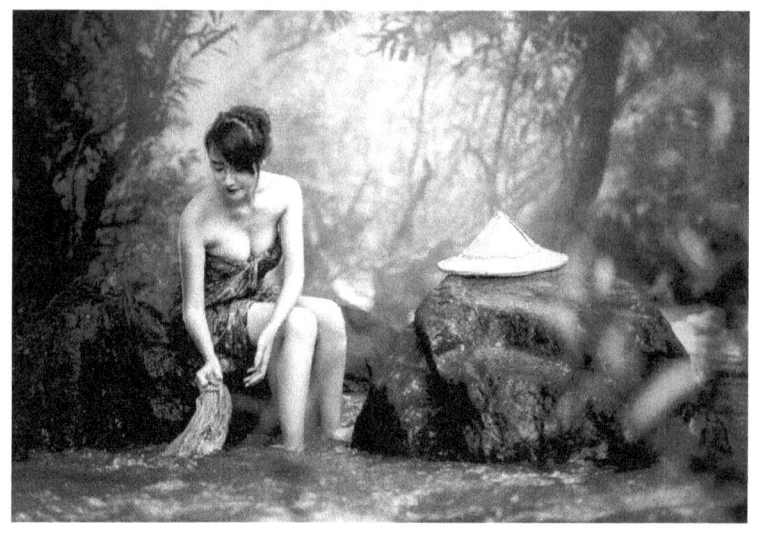

Another great element of DSLR cameras is the video-mode that comes built-in. This is the 11th mode on most cameras, and it is a great mode to have. While taking photographs are incredible, sometimes they don't always capture the whole moment away a short video would. On the other hand, maybe you would like to film an entire moment, but don't have a video camera available to you. For whatever reason you may be interested in using video mode, it can be beneficial to understand how it works, the basics, and how to take high quality videos on your camera. In this chapter, we will introduce you to the video mode on your DSLR, and how to use it properly.

Most modern DSLR cameras have a video mode. There are also HDSLR (High Definition Single Lens Reflex) cameras that have been declared to shoot better quality videos than many moderate-level video cameras. So, it can definitely be a great asset to understand how to use the video mode on your DSLR.

Before you get into the core of learning how to use your DSLR for video, it can be good to understand the pros and cons of working with one for your video projects. This way, you are able to decide if your DSLR is really fit for your project. Below is a list of the best and worst parts about working with a DSLR for videoing:

Pros

- *Can produce high quality footage that looks incredible without needing additional equipment*
- *Work excellent in low-light settings*
- *Smaller and more manageable than many high quality video cameras*
- *Generally cheaper than video cameras*
- *Still use camera lenses, do not require special video lenses*

Cons

- *Can be very hard to achieve a stable video that isn't shaky without using a tripod or other stabilizing equipment - tripods are recommended for the best quality results, therefore it isn't a good idea to use a camera for a film where you are moving the camera around a lot*
- *The sound quality is not as good as it would be with a video camera*
- *If you don't have a good zoom lens, it will be hard to zoom in on your film*
- *When you can zoom in, you can sometimes hear the sound of the zoom-action happening in the video*
- *You cannot zoom in to focus on a specific subject and then zoom out and maintain that focus*
- *You cannot plug in professional microphones to record audio*
- *The viewfinder does not work in video-mode, and the screen can be small and hard to work with*

- *The digital screen is usually inadequate for focusing on your subject effectively, and DSLR's do not have focus-assist options in video mode*
- Some cons that only apply to certain cameras:
- *Some cameras will automatically end your film after a certain amount of time to prevent over heating*
- *Certain cameras don't have a microphone built-in so you must add sound later on*

Even though there are quite a few "cons" to the list, most of them don't apply to people who aren't looking to achieve professional-quality videos with their DSLR cameras. Regardless of the negatives, DSLR camera videos can actually look amazing if done right, and are excellent treasures for families who are looking to maintain and cherish their memories for years to come. If you are interested in learning how to use your DSLR camera to do so, you have come to the right place!

Equipment

There are some equipment pieces that are highly recommended if you are using your DSLR for filming. This equipment is what will make your video high-quality, and worthy of becoming a profound part of your memory files. Most of this equipment will help save you from any headache of not being able to achieve the perfect clips, too.

Extra Battery

Just like with photographing, having an extra battery when filming is incredibly helpful. Videoing on your DSLR tends to use up a lot of battery in a short amount of time, so it is a good idea to have an extra battery handy so you can either continue filming, or continue taking photographs after your first battery runs out of juice. Also, remember to keep both batteries fully charged! Having a dead battery in your arsenal will not help you out when it comes to actually using them!

LED Camera Light

Many places sell LED lights that mount where the flash usually sits, and are used to put light into your video. Since videos don't have the same ability to absorb extra light like long-exposure photos can, you will need to add light if your scene isn't illuminated enough. These lights generally run completely on their own, and are mounted in the same spot a flash is mounted. Most run on camera-style batteries that you purchase with the lights, or come with the lights. Then, you simply mount it and turn it on to the necessary brightness to illuminate your shot. The cool thing about LED camera lights is that they often come with different filters you can put over the lights to change the warmth of the light and make the video have a more desirable light quality to it. It is also recommended that you get an additional battery for your LED light so that you don't end up without a light when you are filming! Again, keep both of them charged so you are never without your backup.

Tripods

There is equipment you can purchase that you wear and you can hold and aim the camera while the equipment holds it perfectly still for you. If you are planning on taking videos where you will be moving around with the camera a lot, this may be worth looking into, but otherwise a simple tripod will do. Having a tripod will allow you to keep the camera perfectly still while filming. Then, you can either set it and leave it, or set it and move the tripod around on its swivel to keep your subject in the shot. If you are going to be doing the latter, make sure that you don't have the screws on your tripod too tight. Otherwise, your camera movements will be jerky and won't look smooth.

Taking the Video

The actual video process is easy. Once you get your equipment in place, it really is as simple as putting it in video mode, focusing on your subject and hitting record. You can then follow your subject and take your film as you wish. Since the actual execution is simple, we won't go into any detailed guides on that portion. However, we will provide you some tips and insight from others who use their DSLR cameras as video cameras. This way, you can implement these tips and make your videos even better!

Plan Your Video

When you are shooting a video, whether with a DSLR or video camera, it can be very beneficial to pre-plan your film before you hit record. While you don't need any professional skills on story-boarding, it can still greatly assist you in planning videos that will make sense chronologically. They will also be easier to edit later on.

Film Like You Photograph

Almost all of the rules that apply to photography apply to filming as well: exposure, composition, balance, subject focus, and other photography tips are still relevant. When you are filming, make sure that your lighting is proper, that your shot is perfectly aligned and that your subject is clearly defined.

Consider Where Your Final Video Will Be Watched

While this may not be as important to people just looking to film home videos, it can still be a good idea to think about. Most cameras shoot in a 4:3 aspect ratio, but most HDTV's require at 16:9 picture. You will need to use either 1020 X 1080, or 1280 X 720 in order to get the type of resolution that is required by these TV monitors. While not all cameras offer this quality, if yours does, you should use it. If it does not, then you just need to be aware that your film may look amazing on the computer, but not so much on a large TV screen.

Shutter Speed

When you are shooting a photograph, having a fast shutter speed helps you freeze the action and get the perfect moment. With filming though, you will want to have your shutter speed lower so that your images blend together seamlessly and you don't end up with a choppy action. However, you also don't want your shutter speed too slow. If it is, your film will start to look sloppy.

Seriously Use Your Tripod

Tripods are a part of the recommended equipment for a reason: without them, you will have a very shaky video that will be hard to watch without feeling dizzy or sick. Instead of having a low-quality, shaky video, use the tripod that is a part of your filming equipment. This way, you can have a stable focus and photograph. If you need to, you can move the camera around on the tripod by unscrewing the tightening screws and gently and gracefully moving the camera around. As previously mentioned, there is other equipment you can use if you will be moving the camera around a lot, and not just in a single spot, but otherwise you shouldn't need to invest in anything more than a simple tripod. If you really don't have one, and you are only shooting for home videos, consider setting your camera down on a flat, stable surface that is level with what you want to take a video of. This way, you get the stability without having to use a tripod. Though, this won't work if your subject will be moving around a lot.

Frame Rates

Generally, DSLR cameras have frame rates for when you're filming. There are three rates typically: 24 frames per second (fps), 30 fps, or 60 fps. Each one can be used for its own specific value, depending on the quality of film you are going for. 24 fps videos have a soft, cinematic air to them. 30 fps films will look the same as broadcast TV does. 60 fps films are excellent for viewing at normal speed, or being slowed down to slo-mo and being viewed at a slower speed, without affecting the video quality. The faster the frame speed, the slower you can make your slo-mo videos without having a jittery effect on your film.

Use That Zoom

Your in-camera zoom may not work on your DSLR, but you can always use your lens to achieve the same affect, assuming you have a zooming lens. It can be very helpful to add depth and focus to your videos if you actually utilize the zoom.

Focus Manually

It might seem easier to allow your camera to automatically control the focus of your film, but the reality is that with a constantly moving target, it will have a hard time picking and maintaining a focus. The best thing to do is to use the manual focus feature and focus your camera on what you want it to focus on. This way, you won't be jumping out of focus every few seconds.

Try a High Quality, Hand-Held Recorder

Many DSLR cameras do not produce high quality audio, especially if there is wind involved. While most of them don't allow you to attach any type of microphone to them, you can still invest in a high quality hand-held recorder to achieve the same affect. Simply turn on the recorder and record the audio at the same time as your camera is recording the film. Then, later when you are editing your film, you can upload the audio and merge the two together so you have a film with audio that actually works together with the film.

Invest in, and Master Editing Software

Just like a major component of photography is editing, it is also a major part of filming. While you typically don't want to edit as much of your video as you might with your photos, it is still important to have a software that is usable, and can help you improve your videos to be incredible instead of just good. Most computers come with editing software pre-installed, but if yours doesn't, there are many inexpensive programs you can invest in that will help you with this. The best idea is to invest in a software and learn to use it properly. Using these software programs, you can merge audio and video together if you are using a separate audio device, you can edit out bad parts, and add cool effects or overlays to your videos.

Record Your Own Tips

Once again, it is a good idea to have a notebook handy when you are practicing filming with your DSLR. Just like with photography, it can be beneficial to write down any of your own tips, tricks or techniques that you pick up while you are filming. This way, you can look back on your notes in the future if you need help troubleshooting, or if you are looking to create high quality videos with lessons you've already learned. Keep this notebook available whenever you are filming so you can easily jot down anything you might want to remember later on.

Conclusion

Thank you so much for reading "Photography for Beginners: *Basic Functions of DSLR Cameras and Taking Quality Photos". This detailed photography book was made to offer you some of the best advice available about photography, and using your DSLR camera. Each chapter was dedicated to helping you become a master with your camera, and create amazing shots while building your photography talent.*

I hope that you were able to become comfortable with your DSLR and practice taking incredible photographs. With this guide, you can learn to photograph just about anything, from family gatherings to beautiful scenery and more. You can also capture short videos with your camera with some excellent tips on how to get the most out of your DSLR video-mode.

The next step is to take this guide, and your camera, and get out there and practice! Remember, a few minutes every day is the best way to become amazing with your camera. The more you use it, the easier it will be for you to really master your DSLR and start taking professional-quality photographs. Also, no photograph is a bad photograph. You either learned some incredible knowledge about how to do better next time, or captured something amazing that you will enjoy for years to come. Have fun, and enjoy yourself while you play around with your new hobby.

Lastly, if you enjoyed reading this book, please take the time to review it on Amazon Kindle. Your honest feedback and opinions would be greatly appreciated.

Thank you, and have fun with your photography ventures!